GREAT PREDATORS

KOMODO
DRAGON

by Patrick G. Cain

Content Consultant
Martha L. (Marty) Crump
Adjunct Professor
Department of Biology
Utah State University

CORE
LIBRARY

Published by ABDO Publishing Company, PO Box 398166, Minneapolis, MN 55439. Copyright © 2014 by Abdo Consulting Group, Inc. International copyrights reserved in all countries. No part of this book may be reproduced in any form without written permission from the publisher. The Core Library™ is a trademark and logo of ABDO Publishing Company.

Printed in the United States of America,
North Mankato, Minnesota
052013
032014
♻ THIS BOOK CONTAINS AT LEAST 10% RECYCLED MATERIALS.

Editor: Lauren Coss
Series Designer: Becky Daum

Library of Congress Control Number: 2013932505

Cataloging-in-Publication Data
Cain, Patrick G.
  Komodo dragon / Patrick G. Cain.
    p. cm. -- (Great Predators)
ISBN 978-1-61783-949-8 (lib. bdg.)
ISBN 978-1-62403-014-7 (pbk.)
Includes bibliographical references and index.
1. Komodo dragon--Juvenile literature. 2. Predatory animals--Juvenile literature. I. Title.
597.95--dc23
                                        2013932505

CONTENTS

CHAPTER ONE

ON THE HUNT

The adult water buffalo is the biggest animal on Komodo Island in Indonesia. It stands nearly six feet (2 m) tall. The beast has five-foot (1.5-m) horns and weighs nearly 2,700 pounds (1,225 kg). The adult water buffalo has little to fear as it grazes the island's grassland. But a hungry Komodo dragon is hiding nearby.

Komodo dragons can kill prey much bigger than they are.

Komodo dragons' long tongues help the lizards sense the world around them.

The Komodo dragon needs to be careful. One kick or blow from the water buffalo's horns could hurt or even kill the ten-foot-long (3-m) lizard. Hunting is a waiting game for the Komodo dragon. The water buffalo can outrun the great predator, so the dragon waits for the water buffalo to walk by. Then the lizard will ambush the water buffalo.

The Komodo dragon's long, yellow, fork-shaped tongue begins flicking out of its mouth. The attack is coming. With each flick, the dragon is reading information in the air. It is seeing and smelling with its tongue. It waits for the water buffalo to draw near.

An Infrequent Eater

Komodo dragons can wait for the right time to attack their prey. The lizard averages just one meal a month. When it does eat, the dragon eats a large amount. In one sitting, the lizard can ingest more than 50 percent of its body weight. If a 100-pound (45-kg) human ate 50 percent of his or her body weight, it would mean eating 50 pounds (23 kg) of food.

The water buffalo walks past the dragon, not seeing the lizard. The Komodo dragon lunges. It bites the water buffalo's ankle with its sharp, serrated teeth. The water buffalo pulls its foot out of the

Komodo dragon's mouth. It limps away with only a small wound. The Komodo dragon waits nearby. The dragons' mouth is full of dangerous bacteria. Those bacteria are at work in the water buffalo's wound. Within a few days, the bacteria will likely kill the water buffalo. Then the Komodo dragon will have its meal.

The Biggest Lizard

Komodo dragons live in the wild on several islands in the country of Indonesia. They are a species of monitor lizard. Monitor lizards are known for their forked tongues and large necks and tails. The Komodo dragon is the world's largest lizard. It can grow up to ten feet (3 m) in length. It can weigh more than 200 pounds (90 kg). The dragon's large tail makes up more than half of its body length. It has short, strong legs. These huge lizards use their sturdy builds to knock down and overpower their prey.

Komodo dragons can run as fast as 13 miles per hour (21 km/h). But they can only keep up this speed for a short time. Instead of chasing down animals,

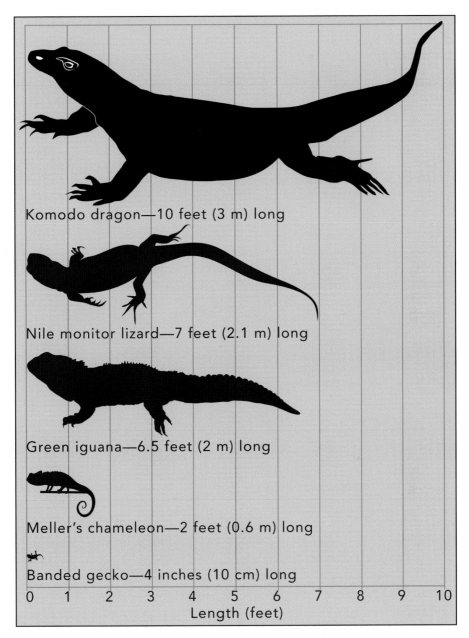

Komodo dragon—10 feet (3 m) long

Nile monitor lizard—7 feet (2.1 m) long

Green iguana—6.5 feet (2 m) long

Meller's chameleon—2 feet (0.6 m) long

Banded gecko—4 inches (10 cm) long

Length (feet)

Large Lizards

This diagram compares the Komodo dragon with other common lizards. After reading about the Komodo dragon, how big did you think it would look? How might its larger size affect the way it hunts compared to smaller lizards?

Discovering a Dragon

People in Indonesia have lived near Komodo dragons for thousands of years. For hundreds of years, sailors reported seeing dragon-like creatures on Indonesian islands. But many people believed the dragons were just a myth. Then in 1910, Dutch lieutenant van Steyn van Hensbroek learned about the dragon. He eventually captured and killed one. This proved the Komodo dragon's existence to Europeans and North Americans.

Komodo dragons usually wait for the right time to ambush their prey. Most adult Komodo dragons are greenish-black or gray. This helps them blend in with trees and grasses so prey do not see them. Like other lizards, a Komodo dragon's skin is covered in scales.

Komodo dragons can be brutal predators. They eat almost any kind of meat. They will attack prey much larger than themselves. They even eat one another.

These big lizards have been known to attack humans. But they are not as fierce as their name suggests. While Komodo dragons are predators,

Komodo dragons are powerful predators, but they also make their dinners out of animals they find already dead.

they are also scavengers. This means they eat the remains of animals that are already dead. In fact they are as likely to eat a dead animal as to try to ambush a live one.

CHAPTER TWO

A DRAGON'S LIFE

Komodo dragons are not social animals. They live most of their lives alone and away from each other. However, they do come together when it is time to mate. Most female Komodo dragons mate when they are about nine years old. Males are ready to mate when they are ten years old.

Most mating takes place in summer. There are three times as many male Komodo dragons as

Komodo dragons are very small when they first hatch from their eggs.

No Male Needed

In 2006 a Komodo dragon named Flora laid 11 eggs at the English zoo where she lived. The eggs were a surprise because Flora had never been in contact with a male Komodo dragon. Flora was one of the first documented cases of a female Komodo dragon laying eggs without having mated. It proved female Komodo dragons do not need males to lay eggs. In January 2007, five healthy Komodo dragons hatched from the eggs. The ability to reproduce without mating is known as parthenogenesis. Scientists have observed this behavior in sharks and several other animals. This trait could be good for the dragons. It could allow a lone female to reproduce even if she swam to or washed up on an island where there were no other Komodo dragons.

females. This is likely because breeding is hard work for the female dragon. She spends up to seven months guarding her eggs. During this time, she hardly eats. When she is finally done guarding the nest, she is very weak. This makes her more vulnerable to disease or attacks by other dragons.

Because there are fewer females, competition for a mate is fierce. Male Komodo dragons wrestle one another to mate with a female. After the battle,

Some Komodo dragons lay their eggs in nests abandoned by megapode birds.

the loser runs away or lies still. The winning dragon approaches the female and licks her with his forked tongue. If she is ready to mate, she licks him back.

In the Egg

Female Komodo dragons usually lay eggs in September. They lay between 15 and 25 eggs. They make nests in sand or decaying plant matter. Some

A baby Komodo dragon walks past unhatched eggs at Surabaya Zoo in Indonesia.

dragons use nests made by megapodes, a bird species native to Indonesia. The nests keep the eggs warm until they are ready to hatch.

Baby Komodo dragons spend between seven and eight months growing and developing in their eggs. The eggs stretch a bit as the Komodo dragons get bigger. A baby Komodo dragon grows a special tooth while inside the egg. This tooth is outside of the dragon's mouth, like a horn. When it is ready to hatch, the Komodo dragon uses this razor-sharp tooth to cut its way out of the shell. The tooth falls out once the dragon is free.

Escaping the egg can be very tiring. Sometimes a Komodo dragon stays inside its broken eggshell to rest for more than a day. Then it is ready for its first meal.

Komodo dragons are ready to hunt almost right away. Most Komodo dragons hatch in April. April is the end of Indonesia's rainy season. Insects are all over the islands. They are the main food for young Komodo dragons.

Growing Up

Mother Komodo dragons usually leave after their babies hatch. Newborn Komodo dragons are approximately 18 inches (46 cm) long. These little

The Largest Dragon

Komodo dragons never stop growing. Usually the older the dragon, the bigger it is. The largest known Komodo dragon lived at the Saint Louis Zoo in Missouri in the 1930s. The lizard was known as Minnie the Dragon Lady. Minnie was 10.3 feet (3.1 m) long and weighed nearly 370 pounds (168 kg).

Young Komodo dragons are more brightly colored than adults. They spend much of their time in trees, where they are safer from hungry adult dragons and other predators.

lizards are easy targets for larger predators. Bigger Komodo dragons eat the babies. Young Komodo dragons spend most of their time in trees, hiding from predators.

Young Komodo dragons are brightly colored. They have greenish-black scales and white and yellow speckles. Their tails have alternating light and dark color bands. This coloration helps camouflage the little lizards in tree leaves.

Young Komodo dragons search tree branches for beetles and other insects to eat. When the Komodo dragons get a bit bigger, they eat bird eggs and smaller lizards. Young Komodo dragons grow fast. In the first few years of its life, a Komodo dragon can double its weight and grow one foot (0.3 m) in length each year.

Once the dragon is approximately three feet (0.9 m) long, it is safe to come down from the trees. It spends the rest of its life on the ground, where its only predators are other Komodo dragons.

CHAPTER THREE

AMAZING PREDATORS

K omodo dragons are strong and fast. Once a Komodo dragon catches its prey, the animal usually does not survive. Komodo dragons do not always eat fresh meat. They are also scavengers. They eat the carcasses of animals they find dead. Komodo dragons use their super senses to track their next meal.

A Komodo dragon uses its tongue to smell the air on an Indonesian savanna.

Smelling with Their Tongues

A Komodo dragon's vision is similar to a human's eyesight. These lizards can see up to 985 feet (300 m) away. They have poor vision in dim light. They also have poor hearing. However, they have an excellent sense of smell. Komodo dragons use this sense in a different way than many other animals.

The Komodo dragon tastes the air with its long tongue. Scientists think this action is a mixture of smelling and tasting. The tongue collects information, such as odors, from air molecules. Then the lizard touches its tongue to an organ on the roof of its mouth. The organ interprets the information for the lizard.

Human Attacks

Komodo dragons have killed few humans. On average, only one attack is reported each year. In 2009 a park ranger was attacked by a Komodo dragon that got into his home. The same ranger was attacked in 2013 when a Komodo dragon got into the national park office where he was working.

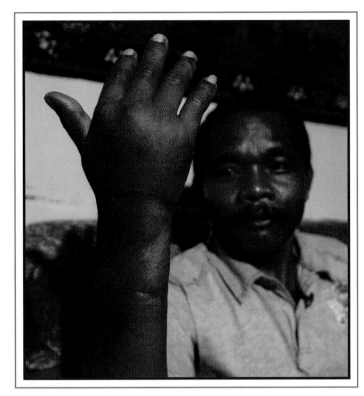

Park ranger Ahmad Main was attacked by Komodo dragons twice between 2009 and 2013, but he survived both attacks.

It tells the dragon how far away objects are and what they might taste like.

Searching for Supper

Komodo dragons are not picky about what they eat. They eat deer, goats, boars, water buffaloes, and other large animals. They also eat smaller animals, such as birds and lizards.

Komodo dragons usually hunt alone, and they are very patient. A lizard will follow the scent of a dead

Dragon Venom

Scientists recently discovered that Komodo dragons have glands in their mouths that produce venom. This venom may contribute to killing the dragons' prey. Scientists need more research to be certain of the role this venom plays in a Komodo dragon's attack. But the venom may work with the dragon's bacteria to kill wounded prey.

animal for a long time. Komodo dragons hide and ambush live prey as the animal walks by. They often attack animals while they are sleeping for an easier kill.

Komodo dragons try to kill their prey right away. The lizard has more than 60 razor-sharp teeth. Each tooth is about one and one-half inches (3.8 cm) long. These teeth fall out easily, but they grow back in a few months. The lizard uses its teeth to bite and tear into its prey's flesh.

However, even if the prey escapes the Komodo dragon, the lizard will not wait long for its meal. Because they eat so much carrion, Komodo dragons have many kinds of dangerous bacteria living inside

Komodo dragons would much rather ambush their prey than chase it down. The lizards often hide along trails where animals are likely to pass by.

their mouths. Once the Komodo dragon bites its prey, the bacteria usually kill the animal within a week.

After the Kill

A Komodo dragon's sharp teeth are not good for chewing. The lizard rips off pieces of meat and swallows them whole. In fact the lizard can swallow an entire goat.

Komodo dragons eat bones, hooves, and fur. They spit up anything they are not able to digest.

Many Komodo dragons will often share the same meal.

Depending on the animal, these lizards may leave only about 12 percent of their prey uneaten.

Komodo dragons may hunt alone, but they often share their meal. Bigger Komodo dragons can take down animals many times their size. This means there are often plenty of scraps for smaller Komodo dragons. But if a smaller lizard is not careful, it may become part of the meal.

An Associated Press article from 2009 discusses Indonesian villagers' views on the dragons:

> [Villagers] say they've always lived peacefully with Komodos. A popular traditional legend tells of a man who once married a dragon "princess." Their twins, a human boy, Gerong, and a lizard girl, Orah, were separated at birth.
>
> When Gerong grew up, the story goes, he met a fierce-looking beast in the forest. But just as he was about to spear it, his mother appeared, revealing to him that the two were brother and sister.
>
> "How could the dragons get so aggressive? . . . They never used to attack us when we walked alone in the forest, or attack our children," [Indonesian resident Haji Amin] said. "We're all really worried about this."

Source: Irwan Firdaus, Associated Press. "Komodo Dragon Attacks Terrorize Villages." NBC News. NBCNews.com, May 24, 2009. Web. Accessed March 11, 2013.

Changing Minds

This passage discusses how Indonesian villagers feel about Komodo dragons. Reread the passage. Do you think the villagers should be afraid of Komodo dragons? Write a short paragraph explaining your opinion.

ISLAND PREDATORS

Komodo dragons only live on the Indian Ocean islands of Komodo, Rinca, Gili Motang, and Flores. Together these islands are half the size of Rhode Island. This is the smallest range of any large predator in the world.

A Tropical Home

The Komodo dragons' home islands all belong to the same country, Indonesia. Indonesia is an archipelago,

Komodo dragons have a very small range. In the wild, they are only found on a handful of Indonesian islands.

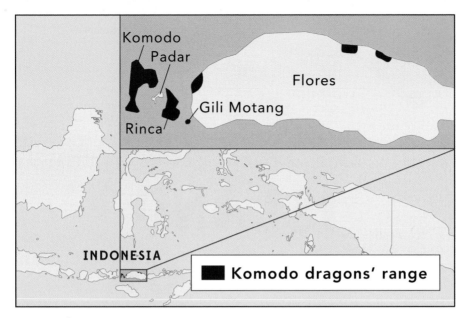

Komodo Dragon Range
This map shows the range of the Komodo dragon. Why might Komodo dragons have evolved in these areas? What natural barriers might prevent the lizards from spreading to other regions? How might living in such a small area affect the Komodo dragon population?

or a group of islands. These islands are all near the equator, so the climate is very warm. The average temperature is 81 degrees Fahrenheit (27°C). Each year the islands average nearly 70 inches (178 cm) of rain.

Komodo dragons need warm weather. They are cold-blooded. This means their body temperature changes depending on the surrounding temperature.

The lizards lie in the sun to keep warm in cooler weather. Komodo dragons usually hunt in daylight. They need the sun to warm their bodies so they have the energy they need for hunting.

After coming down from the trees, young Komodo dragons usually live in grasslands or low forests. The lizards dig small dens in the ground where they can sleep and rest. Some dragons spend a great deal of time on beaches, eating dead animals that wash up on shore.

Losing a Home

At one time, Komodo dragons lived on the Indonesian island of Padar. However, in the 1970s and 1980s, deer and wild boar were hunted heavily on the island. The deer and boar were some of the Padar dragons' main sources of prey. As the deer and boar populations declined, so did the Komodo dragon populations. Some hunters lit wildfires on the island to drive animals into the open. These fires burned much of the dragons' habitat. The reduced habitat and prey could not sustain the dragons left on the island. By 2000 Komodo dragons were extinct on Padar.

Komodo dragons spend much of their day resting in the sun to warm their bodies.

The Komodo dragon is a threatened species. This means its future is in jeopardy. The reason the dragon's population is limited is partly because the area where they live is so small. Scientists believe there are approximately 4,000 dragons left in the wild.

EXPLORE ONLINE

Chapter Four discusses Komodo dragons' range and habitat. Many Komodo dragons currently live in Komodo National Park. The Web site below discusses Komodo National Park. As you know, every source is different. How is the information on the Web site different from this chapter? How is it the same?

Komodo National Park
www.mycorelibrary.com/komodo-dragon

CHAPTER FIVE

THE DRAGONS' FUTURE

Komodo dragons have walked the earth for millions of years. But they may not be here forever. The species is threatened. The Komodo dragons' population is so small that the species is at risk of becoming extinct.

One of the major problems for Komodo dragons' survival is their location. The lizards live on only a few tiny islands. The dragon populations are highly

Human development is one of the biggest threats to Komodo dragons. It can also put the lizards in more frequent contact with humans, which can be dangerous for both humans and dragons.

Population Max

Komodo dragons are threatened because their range is so small. Yet some scientists think the dragon population on Komodo Island is about as big as it can get. The island does not have enough resources to support a larger population.

impacted whenever human development or natural disasters happen on these islands.

Threats to the Komodo Dragon

Adult Komodo dragons have no natural predators. For a long time, they only needed to fear other Komodo dragons. However, in recent years, humans have put these predators' future at risk.

The Indonesian government has taken steps to protect the lizard's habitat. In 1980 the government created Komodo National Park to protect part of the Komodo dragon's home. The park includes the islands of Komodo, Rinca, and Gili Motang along with many other islands.

Laws are in place to protect Komodo dragons. Some people still poach, or illegally hunt and kill,

Komodo National Park helps protect the giant monitor lizards from hunting and habitat loss.

the large lizards. Many people fear Komodo dragons since they occasionally attack humans. Villagers sometimes put poisoned meat out for the lizards to eat. They hope to keep Komodo dragons away from their homes and villages.

Protecting the Komodo dragon means protecting its prey. Without food to hunt, the dragon cannot survive. Poaching deer and other animals the Komodo dragon eats still takes place in Komodo National Park.

To ensure Komodo dragons' survival, humans must find a way to coexist with the lizards.

With fewer prey to eat, Komodo dragons are more likely to eat one another.

Komodo dragons also face habitat loss. On the island of Flores, humans cut down the forests in a destructive way. This left the lizard with fewer places to live. Now the Komodo dragon lives in only a few small areas on the island.

In 2009 people began gold mining on Komodo Island. The mine was just 12 miles (19 km) from Komodo National Park. Some people worried the mining would threaten the 2,500 Komodo dragons living in the park. Environmentalists wanted the Indonesian government to help by closing the mine. They also wanted the government to take greater steps to protect the lizards from poachers.

Important Predators

The Komodo dragon's future depends on humans to do their part to protect the world's environment. Komodo dragons are very important predators on their island homes. If the number of Komodo dragons decreases, the populations of their prey will increase. There will be more animals competing for the same resources

Climate Change

One of the newest problems to face Komodo dragons is rising sea levels. Most scientists agree the earth's average temperature is slowly rising. Right now, sea ice is trapped at the North and South Poles. These areas are known as the polar ice caps. Rising temperatures are causing the polar ice caps to melt. If enough ice melts, it will raise sea levels around the world. Island countries would likely lose land to the ocean, making the areas where Komodo dragons live even smaller than they are today.

Komodo dragons play an important role on their island homes.

on the island. Eventually, the prey populations may decrease as well if food becomes too scarce. This could put some species at risk of extinction.

Komodo dragons help keep their ecosystems balanced by keeping prey populations from becoming too large. It is important for humans to find ways to protect these amazing animals and live alongside them.

In 2007 a group of scientists published a paper about the possible effects of climate change on Indonesia:

The combination of high population density and high levels of biodiversity . . . makes Indonesia one of the most vulnerable countries to the impacts of climate change. . . . Impacts of observed changes in climate are already evident in Indonesia and will likely worsen due to further human-induced climate change. Rising concentrations of greenhouse gases will continue to raise the surface and ocean temperatures, change precipitation patterns, increase sea levels, and cause various other impacts from more frequent forest fires to increased health risks. Climate change will also continue to affect "natural" climate variability, such as El Niño, and may lead to more frequent and more intense weather events.

Source: Michael Case, Fitrian Ardiansyah, and Emily Spector. "Climate Change in Indonesia: Implications for Humans and Nature." World Wildlife Federation. WWF, 2007. PDF. 3. Web. Accessed March 12, 2013.

Back It Up

The authors of this passage use evidence to support a main point. Write a paragraph describing the point the authors are making. Then write down two or three pieces of evidence the authors use to make that point.

Common Name: Komodo dragon

Scientific Name: *Varanus komodoensis*

Average Size: Eight feet (2.4 m) for adults

Average Weight: 100 pounds (45 kg)

Color: Greenish-black with white and yellow speckles when young; greenish-black or gray as adults

Average Lifespan: 30 years

Diet: Any kind of meat, including deer, water buffaloes, boars, other Komodo dragons, and carrion

Habitat: Grasslands and low forests on the Indonesian islands of Komodo, Rinca, Gili Motang, and Flores

Predators: Other Komodo dragons and humans

Did You Know?

- A Komodo dragon can eat more than 50 percent of its body weight in a single sitting.
- A Komodo dragon can swallow an animal as large as a goat whole.
- Komodo dragons smell with their tongues.

Dig Deeper

After reading this book, what questions do you still have about Komodo dragons? Do you want to learn more about their diet? Or their habitat? Write down one or two questions to guide your research. With an adult's help, find a few reliable sources about Komodo dragons to help answer these questions. Write a few sentences about how you did your research and what you learned from it.

Why Do I Care?

Komodo dragons are very important predators for their ecosystems. You might live far away from Komodo dragons' home islands, but you can still help protect these lizards by doing your part to help reduce climate change. Write an essay explaining ways people in other parts of the world can help protect these predators.

Tell the Tale

Chapter One describes a Komodo dragon in action. Write 200 words telling the story of a Komodo dragon ambushing its prey. Describe what the Komodo dragon sees and smells. Make sure to set the scene, develop a sequence of events, and write a conclusion.

Surprise Me

Learning about new animals can be interesting and surprising. After reading this book, what two or three facts about Komodo dragons did you find most surprising? Write a few sentences about each fact. Why did you find it surprising?

GLOSSARY

ambush
a surprise attack from a hiding place

archipelago
a group of islands

carrion
dead and rotting flesh

ecosystem
the group of plants and animals living in and interacting with their environment

extinct
a species that has completely died out

parthenogenesis
the ability to reproduce without mating

poach
collect or hunt an animal illegally

scavenger
an animal that eats animals that are already dead

serrated
with notches like the teeth of a saw

species
a group of similar animals that are closely related enough to mate with one another

venom
poison produced by an animal

LEARN MORE

Books

Crump, Marty. *Mysteries of the Komodo Dragon: The Biggest, Deadliest Lizard Gives Up Its Secrets*. Honesdale, PA: Boyds Mill Press, 2010.

Cumming, David. *Indonesia*. North Mankato, MN: Cherrytree Books, 2004.

Hamilton, Sue. *Lizards*. Edina, MN: ABDO, 2010.

Web Links

To learn more about Komodo dragons, visit ABDO Publishing Company online at **www.abdopublishing.com**. Web sites about Komodo dragons are featured on our Book Links page. These links are routinely monitored and updated to provide the most current information available.
Visit **www.mycorelibrary.com** for free additional tools for teachers and students.

INDEX

ABOUT THE AUTHOR

Patrick G. Cain is a freelance writer, designer, and former nuclear engineer. His written works can be found in outlets from *ESPN* to *Women's Health*.